SNAIL (WHITE) ¥378
PAPERWEIGHT OR CHOPSTICK HOLDER
HIPPO (WHITE) ¥378
PAPERWEIGHT OR CHOPSTICK HOLDER
HORSE (BLACK) ¥378
PAPERWEIGHT OR CHOPSTICK HOLDER
BUNNY (WHITE) ¥378
PAPERWEIGHT OR CHOPSTICK HOLDER
SHIRAHOSHI KUROE (18)
THANK YOU VERY MUCH!
SALE
SALE

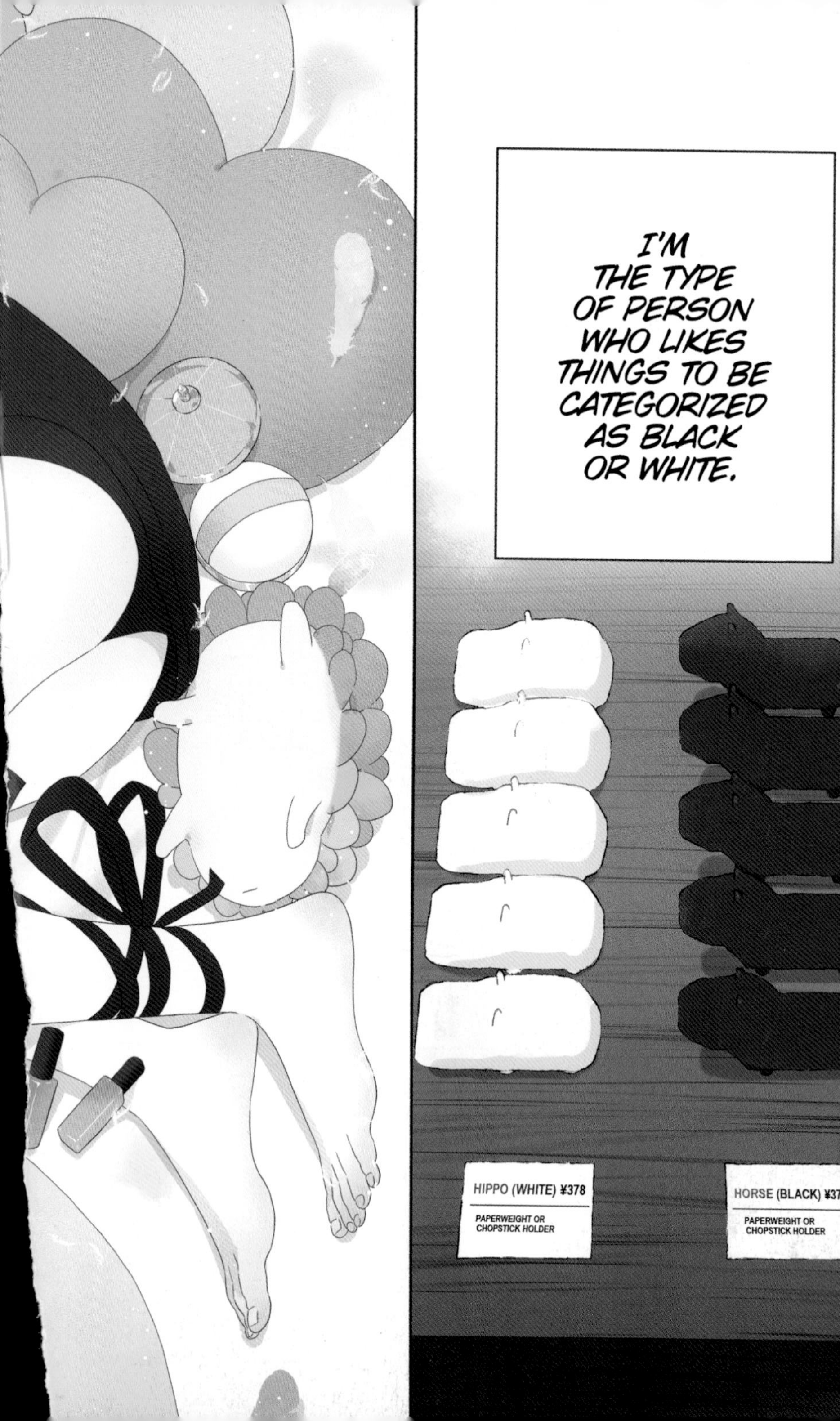
I'M THE TYPE OF PERSON WHO LIKES THINGS TO BE CATEGORIZED AS BLACK OR WHITE.
HIPPO (WHITE) ¥378
PAPERWEIGHT OR CHOPSTICK HOLDER
HORSE (BLACK) ¥378
PAPERWEIGHT OR CHOPSTICK HOLDER

Rainbow and Black (1)
Story & Art by
Eri Takenashi
Ayurveda
white lily
Body oil
#1 The Pickup

CONTENTS

WHAT THE HELL IS WRONG...

WITH MAKING THINGS BLACK AND WHITE?!!

だー
WHITE
だー
WHITE
だー…
WHITE…

PHEW...

I SHOULD GO HOME...

I'M NOT WRONG.
I'M NOT WRONG.

EVERY-ONE ELSE AROUND ME WAS WRONG ...!

TOMORROW'S NOT THE TRASH DAY FOR BULKY ITEMS...
BUT SOMEONE THREW ONE OUT!
THERE ARE SO MANY THINGS WRONG IN THIS WORLD!
THAT'S WHY I CAN'T HELP POINTING OUT THE FAULTS!

A RAINBOW-COLORED...

FURBALL.

NO, FEATHERS.

SHUFFLE
SHUFFLE
IT'S MOVING. IT'S ALIVE.
WHAT AM I SUPPOSED TO DO IN THIS SITUATION?
CALL THE POLICE, SINCE IT'S LOST PROPERTY ...?
......
MAYBE THE OWNER WILL COME BACK FOR IT.
I SHOULD STAY NEXT TO IT FOR A BIT.
......
YOU'VE GOT IT ROUGH, TOO.

NOOO.

NOT REEEALLY.

?!

NO.

IT'S... NOT A BIRD.
IT HAS FOUR LEGS.
IT DOESN'T HAVE A BEAK.
ACTUALLY, WHAT KIND OF MOUTH IS THAT...?
SUU
NOSTRILS... LOOKS LIKE IT HAS NOSTRILS.

WHAT IS THIS?

WHAT ARE YOU?!
WHAT ARE YOU?!

YOU'RE NOT A BIRD, RIGHT?!
YOU'RE NOT A BIRD, RIIIGHT?!

OH...
OKAY. OKAY, OKAY, OKAY...

YOU'RE ONE OF THOSE?
YOU'RE ONE OF THOEZ.
YOU'RE USING MIMICRY, RIGHT?
YOU'RE USING MIMIKRI WRIGHT.
LIKE A PARROT.
LAIK A PAWWOT.

OH... I GET IT NOW.
IT'S NOT A BIRD...
BUT IT'S SOMETHING LIKE A BIRD...!

YOU TALK A LOT.
YOU TALK A LOT.

AREN'T YOU COLD?
NOOO. NOT REEEALLY.
AMAZING. IT'S LIKE A CONVER-SATION.

I SEE. IT'S A BIRD... OR LIKE A BIRD? HUNH.
SHAKE
LOOKING AT THE COLORS OF ITS FEATHERS, IT MUST BE A TROPICAL SPECIES.
IS IT OKAY IN THIS COLD?

I CAN'T JUST LEAVE IT HERE.
I'LL WAIT A BIT LONGER.
THEN I'LL CALL THE POLICE.
AND I'LL TAKE IT HOME FOR NOW.

WELCOME HOME, KURO.

WHAT IS THAT... THING?

I'M HOME, MOM.

I WONDER ...?

DO YOU KNOW WHAT IT IS?

SIGH... SO, YOU ALREADY REPORTED IT...

IT FEELS BETTER TO LOOK AT THINGS LIKE THIS IN BLACK AND WHITE.

......

YOU KNOW, THERE *ARE* COLORS BETWEEN BLACK AND WHITE.

SO...
WHAT ARE YOU GOING TO DO NOW?
WE'RE GOING TO TAKE CARE OF IT...
FOR A WEEK, UNTIL THE PREVIOUS OWNER IS FOUND.
DO YOU KNOW HOW TO TAKE CARE OF IT...?
THAT'S WHAT THE IN-TERNET IS FOR.
RAIN...
BOW...
COL...
ORED...
FUR...
BALL.
oogle search
Rai
Results (18)
Searching for "Rainbow"
TEN IMAGES OF YARN... FIVE IMAGES OF FUR CHARMS...
I HAD A FEELING THAT WOULDN'T WORK...
WHAT SHOULD I SEARCH FOR?
"RARE ANIMAL."
"PET."
"UN-USUAL."
"BIRD."
"FOUR-LEGGED."
"WINGS" ...
HM? WHAT'S THIS?
Is there an animal that has four legs that also has feathers?
Agreed
0
20XX/12/08 18:56
129
4
Best Answer
Best Answer
hjj********san
A famous example would be a "happy mouse."
Likes
0
Report Abuse
I FOUND SOMETHING ON ANSWERS, BUT I WONDER IF IT'S LEGITIMATE.
"HAPPY MOUSE"?
I DON'T THINK IT'S A MOUSE.
OR MAYBE IT IS?

Rainbow-colored Heavenly

All
Images
Movies
Shopping

Rainbow-colored Heavenly Parrot
Animal

THAT'S IT!

PHEW... THERE IT IS!!

THANK GOODNESS! I FOUND IT.

NOW I'LL KNOW WHAT IT EATS.

......

PARROT?

IT'S A TYPE OF PARROT?

Rainbow-colored Heavenly Parrot

Rainbow-colored Heavenly Parrot, also known as Happy Mouse, is the only one of its species in the class Mammalia/Aves and the order Rainbow-colored Heavenly Parrot. Though it has the word "parrot" in its name, it is not genetically similar to true parrots. There is debate on its true scientific classification.

Rainbow-colored Heav

Morphology

Their average height is about
Capable. Colorful feathers (fe
They do not have wings and
Excretions from their unique

Mainly use their front limbs
diet.

They do not have beaks
possible to grab with
ming is used.

After laying their eggs

ssification

ginally classified similarly to
e platypus, due to its egg-layin
cientists have recently debated
hether they are descended fro
inosaurs, similar to modern
birds. This is the current popula
belief, however, the truth rema
a mystery.

Due to possible evolutionary
convergence, the family tree
monkey, mouse, bird are all
options considered the
"creationist's nightmare."

I DON'T ...
GET IT!
NOT A MOUSE OR A BIRD?!
THEY DON'T EVEN KNOW...
HOW IT'S CLASSIFIED?!
ニジイロ
WHAT'S SUCH A RARE CREATURE DOING IN MY NEIGHBORHOOD?
Rainbow-colored H
All
Images
HAHAHA Do you want
Stop! Stop!!

C-COULD IT BE ILLEGAL TO HAVE THEM IN JAPAN?!
SINCE THE POLICE DIDN'T SAY ANYTHING, IT'S PROBABLY FINE.
IT'S A "RARE ANIMAL" IN JAPAN IS ALL THAT MEANS.
CREATURES LIKE AXOLOTLS, SPOTTED GARDEN EELS, AND CAPYBARA...
WERE ALSO CONSIDERED RARE ANIMALS IN THE PAST.
THE INTERNET'S A GOOD TOOL, BUT DON'T BELIEVE EVERYTHING YOU READ.
IF YOU FIND INFORMATION FROM A SKETCHY SITE, WE MIGHT END UP ACCIDENTALLY KILLING IT.
FOR NOW, WE SHOULD JUST WATCH OVER IT CAREFULLY.
ANIMALS OFTEN GET STRESSED WHEN THEIR ENVIRON-MENT CHANGES.
THEY MIGHT CAUSE A RUCKUS OR GET SICK.
FOR NOW, WARM IT UP AND GIVE IT SOME WATER.
ALL ANIMALS DRINK WATER.
DASH

ORAAH!
ORAAAAAAAH!
WHAT IS GOING ON?
IS IT TAUNTING US?
IT'S LIKE THAT EVERY TIME I TRY TO TOUCH IT.
IT DOESN'T LIKE ME AT ALL.
OH, JEEZ. WHAT'S WRONG, LITTLE GUY?
NOW, NOW.
DON'T BE SCARED.
POKE...

WHAT'S WITH *THAT* REACTION?
HUH?
DOES IT LIKE ME?
PRESS...
WHAT DOES THIS BODY LANGUAGE MEAN?
MAYBE IT'S ASKING YOU TO TOUCH IT?

MOM...
CAN I LET IT OUT?
FIDGET...
OH, I'LL LEAVE THE ROOM!
BE CAREFUL!

GA-CHAK

PAD
PAD
PAD
SCAN
SCAN
SHAKE
FLUFF
PLOP

POOP.

AMAZ-ING!
IT GOT ONTO SOME OLD NEWS-PAPERS ON ITS OWN...
AND IT EVEN RE-PORTED THE DEED!
AMAZING !!
NOO! NOT REEEALLY!
YES! AMAZ-ING!

AMAZ-ING!

AMAZING!

MAU MAU...

U-UM...
I'D LIKE TO LEARN ABOUT...
HOW TO RAISE...
A RAINBOW-COLORED HEAVENLY PARROT.
YES. UM...
WE HAVEN'T DECIDED TO KEEP IT, BUT WE'RE CURRENTLY TAKING CARE OF IT.
NO, UM... I FOUND IT.
YES.
YES.
THAT'S RIGHT.
UM!
IT SEEMS THERE AREN'T MANY PEOPLE WHO OWN THEM IN JAPAN.
THERE ARE NO PROBLEMS WITH KEEPING IT, ARE THERE?!
THAT'S NOT A PROBLEM AT ALL.
IT'S JUST THAT THERE AREN'T VERY MANY IN JAPAN.
THERE AREN'T MANY VET-ERINARIANS THAT CAN EXAMINE THEM, EITHER.

TAKING CARE OF THEM...ISN'T ACTUALLY THAT HARD.
THEY HAVE DOCILE PERSONALITIES AND DON'T NEED A LOT OF EXERCISE.
BUT THEY ARE A RARE ANIMAL SPECIES.
THEY ALSO TEND TO GET OFF-BALANCE NUTRITION-ALLY.
NUTRITION...
WHAT SHOULD I FEED IT?
FIFTY PERCENT FRUITS, VEGETABLES, AND GRAINS. TWENTY PERCENT PROTEIN...
CAN I GET YOUR FAX OR EMAIL? I CAN SEND YOU SOME INFO.
WE'RE JUST TAKING CARE OF IT FOR A WEEK, UNTIL THE OWNER IS FOUND...
IT WOULD BE NICE IF THE INGREDIENTS WERE THINGS I COULD GET NEARBY.
I DON'T THINK THAT WILL BE A PROBLEM.
YOU CAN EVEN SWAP IN CAT FOOD OR DOG FOOD.
BUT I CAN'T BELIEVE ANYONE WOULD ABANDON A HAPPY MOUSE...
I'VE NEVER HEARD OF THAT HAPPENING.
PLEASE DON'T HESITATE TO CONTACT ME WITH ANY OTHER QUESTIONS.
I'LL DO MY BEST TO ANSWER THEM.

ALL RIGHT.
WHILE IT'S STAYING HERE...
I'LL TAKE GOOD CARE OF IT.

BUT THE RESPONSIBILITY MIGHT BE TOO MUCH FOR ME.
I MAY HAVE TO START LOOKING FOR A NEW OWNER.

VREE

HUH?! YOU GOT FIRED FROM YOUR PART-TIME JOB?!
OH... I FORGOT TO TELL YOU.
WHY DIDN'T YOU TELL ME RIGHT AWAY?!
THINGS WERE REALLY CRAZY!

NOO. NOT REEEALLY.
WHY DID IT SAY THAT?
IT PROBABLY LEARNED IT FROM ITS PREVIOUS OWNER.

ZZZ

VIBRANTLY COLORED FEATHERS.
FLUFFY.

IT BLINKS.

ITS LEGS.
THEY'RE SO SQUISHY.
PRESS
IT HAS CLAWS ON ITS FEET.

IT'S WARM.
I CAN FEEL ITS HEART BEATING.
I HAVE NO IDEA WHERE IT CAME FROM.
IN THE SCIENTIFIC SENSE, TOO.
BUT YOU'RE ALIVE.
YOU'RE ALIIIVE.
OOPS.
WRIGGLE WRIGGLE
IT MUST BE SCARY TO BE HELD UP SO HIGH.
I'LL PUT YOU DOWN NOW.

OH?
TA-TAK!

WHAT ARE YOU DOING NOW?
TA-TAK!

HUH?
SWAY
SWAY
WHY ARE YOU MOVING LIKE THAT?

ARE YOU DANCING ...?
TEE HEE.

SWIP.....
FWFF...

HOP
HOP
HOP
HOP
HOP
HEE...!
HOP
HOP
HOP
HEE...!
HOP
HOP
A MYSTERIOUS...
DANCE.
PA-PING ♪
Time Skip Slow Video Picture Scroll
......

GA-CHAK
RIIING
RIIING
HELLO?
OH, IT'S YOU.
DID YOU HAVE ANOTHER QUESTION FOR ME?

OH. YES, YES. YOU'RE LOOKING FOR A NEW HOME FOR IT.
FIRST...
GOOD JOB TAKING CARE OF IT FOR A WEEK.

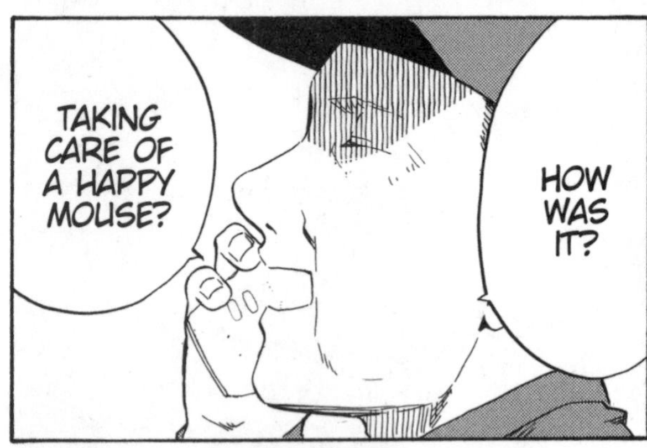

THAT'S WHAT MAKES A HAPPY MOUSE SO LOVABLE.
THEY'VE EVOLVED WITH A HIGH LEVEL OF COMMUNICATION SKILLS AND CAN EASILY BECOME LIFETIME PARTNERS FOR HUMANS.
IF IT GETS CLOSER TO YOU, IT WILL START DANCING OR SINGING FOR YOU.
YES!
I'VE ALREADY SEEN IT DANCE.
OH?
IT RUFFLED UP ALL ITS FEATHERS TO FRAME ITS FACE ...
AND STARTED HOPPING AROUND.
I WAS SO SURPRISED THAT I TOOK A VIDEO OF IT.
....
??
YOU'RE PLANNING TO FIND A NEW HOME FOR IT NOW, RIGHT?
YES?
I WOULDN'T DO THAT IF I WERE YOU.
HAPPY MICE... CHOOSE ONE PARTNER FOR THEIR ENTIRE LIFE.
THEIR LOVE FOR ONE ANOTHER IS VERY DEEP.
IF THEY GET SEPARATED FROM THEIR CHOSEN PARTNER...

THEY'LL PULL OUT THEIR OWN FEATHERS ...
SELF-HARM

STOP EATING ANY FOOD...
FASTING

AND DIE.

THAT DANCE.
IT WAS A COURTSHIP DANCE.

I...
I'M A HUMAN.
THEY SOMETIMES DO IT TOWARDS HUMANS, TOO.
THEY CAN END UP FALLING IN LOVE.

THAT'S THE KIND OF ANIMAL THEY ARE! THAT'S WHY SOME PEOPLE LOVE THEM SO MUCH EVEN THOUGH THEY CAN BE A CHALLENGE.
UM... I KNOW THIS IS GOING TO SOUND A LITTLE STRANGE...
BUT PLEASE, FOR THAT CREATURE'S SAKE...
WON'T YOU KEEP IT...?
I'M ASKING YOU FOR ITS SAKE.
PLEASE...
GASP
LIFE-SPAN!
THE LIFE OF A HAPPY MOUSE ...!
HOW LONG IS IT?!
EIGHTY YEARS.

A NAME ...
I HAVE TO THINK OF ONE.
HUH ?!
WEREN'T YOU GOING TO FIND AN OWNER FOR IT?

LOOKS LIKE FINDING AN OWNER WON'T WORK. I'VE GOTTA KEEP IT.
MY.
SO...
WE'RE GOING TO KEEP IT HERE?

RAIN-BOW.
COLORED.
HEAVENLY PARROT...
SO, THEN.

NIJI.
POINT

I NAME THEE NIJI.

AH HA HA! THE WORD FOR "RAINBOW"!

HUH?
WHY?
HOW DID THIS BECOME ABOUT ME?
WHO KNOOOWS ~?
WHO KNOOOWS ~?
STOP BEING EVASIVE!
SHIRAHOSHI KUROE.
SHE'S THE TYPE WHO LIKES THINGS CLEARLY SPELLED OUT IN BLACK AND WHITE.

Rainbow and Black

Story & Art by Eri Takenashi

NOW LOADING...

#2 Bathing

AH HA HA.
PATTER PATTER PATTER
TOTTER TOTTER TOTTER
PATTER PATTER PATTER
MOM IS PLAYING WITH NIJI.
WHAT IS IT?
WHERE ARE YOU GOING?
THERE?
PATTER PATTER
TOTTER TOTTER TOTTER
SCRATCH SCRATCH SCRATCH
PATTER PATTER
RATTLE
NO, THAT'S--
KURO'S TAKING A BATH!
HUH?
YOU WANT TO JOIN HER?
BANG
KURO!
KURO!
SPLASH
BANG

BANG
BANG
KURO! HEY!
IT KNOWS WHERE YOU ARE, KURO!
IT'S SO SMART!
HEY, ARE YOU LISTENING, KURO?
KURO!
KURO!
KURO——!

KURO!
BANG
KURO!
KURO—!
BANG
BANG
AH HA HA! IT REMEMBERED YOUR NAME!
IT'S SO FREAKING SMART!
AH HA HA!
KURO!
KURO!
BANG
BANG
BANG
KURO!
KURO—!!

KURO—!
KURO—!
KURO—!
KURO——!!!
YEEK...
IT'S...GONNA...ASSAULT...ME!!
YOU'RE OVER-REACTING.
IT'S JUST A BIRD.
SHOULD I LET IT IN?
MAYBE IT WANTS TO BATHE.
WAH!
WAH!
WHOA!

HUH?
SEARCH
WHAT ARE YOU TRYING TO DO?
HUH?
SEARCH
WHOA!
WHOA! YOU'RE CLIMBING UP.
WHOA! HOLD ON.
AAAAAAAH!

WHOA.
YIKES.
PAT PAT
SPLASH
SPLASH
ZA-PLASH
Y-YOU'LL DROWN!
OR WILL YOU ...?
CAN YOU SWIM?
GENTLY...
CHLUP

SHAKE

SHAKE

SHAKE

IT'S BATHING.

LOOKS LIKE IT.

WHY DON'T YOU JUST FINISH YOUR BATH TO-GETHER?

THEN YOU DON'T HAVE TO BOTHER WASHING IT SEPA-RATELY.

HUNH... IS THAT REALLY OKAY?

I'VE NEVER HEARD OF DOING THAT WITH A PET.

JUST LET IT JOIN YOU FOR A BIT.

HA
PLUP
IT LOOKS LIKE...
IT FEELS REALLY GOOD.
ROLL
ROLL
SHAKE SHAKE
IT'S LIKE IT'S USED TO BATHING LIKE THIS.
MAYBE THIS IS HOW IT ALWAYS BATHES?

IT CAN SWIM!
PLASH
PLASH
KURO!
KURO! STOP!
HUH?

● **Make sure to bathe birds in cool water!**

Please use room-temperature water when bathing your bird. Do not use hot water. If you use hot water, it will melt the oil that protects their feathers.

SWELTER...
SPORTS

HUFF! HUFF!
OH? DID WE MAKE IT *TOO* WARM?

WE SHOULD KEEP YOU WARM TONIGHT.
WE'LL TAKE YOU TO THE HOSPITAL TOMORROW.

I'M SORRY... I'M SO SORRY, NIJI.
REALLY... I'M SUCH A WORTHLESS PET OWNER.
REALLY.
A WORTHLESS PET OWNER.
YOU REPEAT MY WORDS WITH SUCH ACCURACY... YOU'RE REALLY SMART.

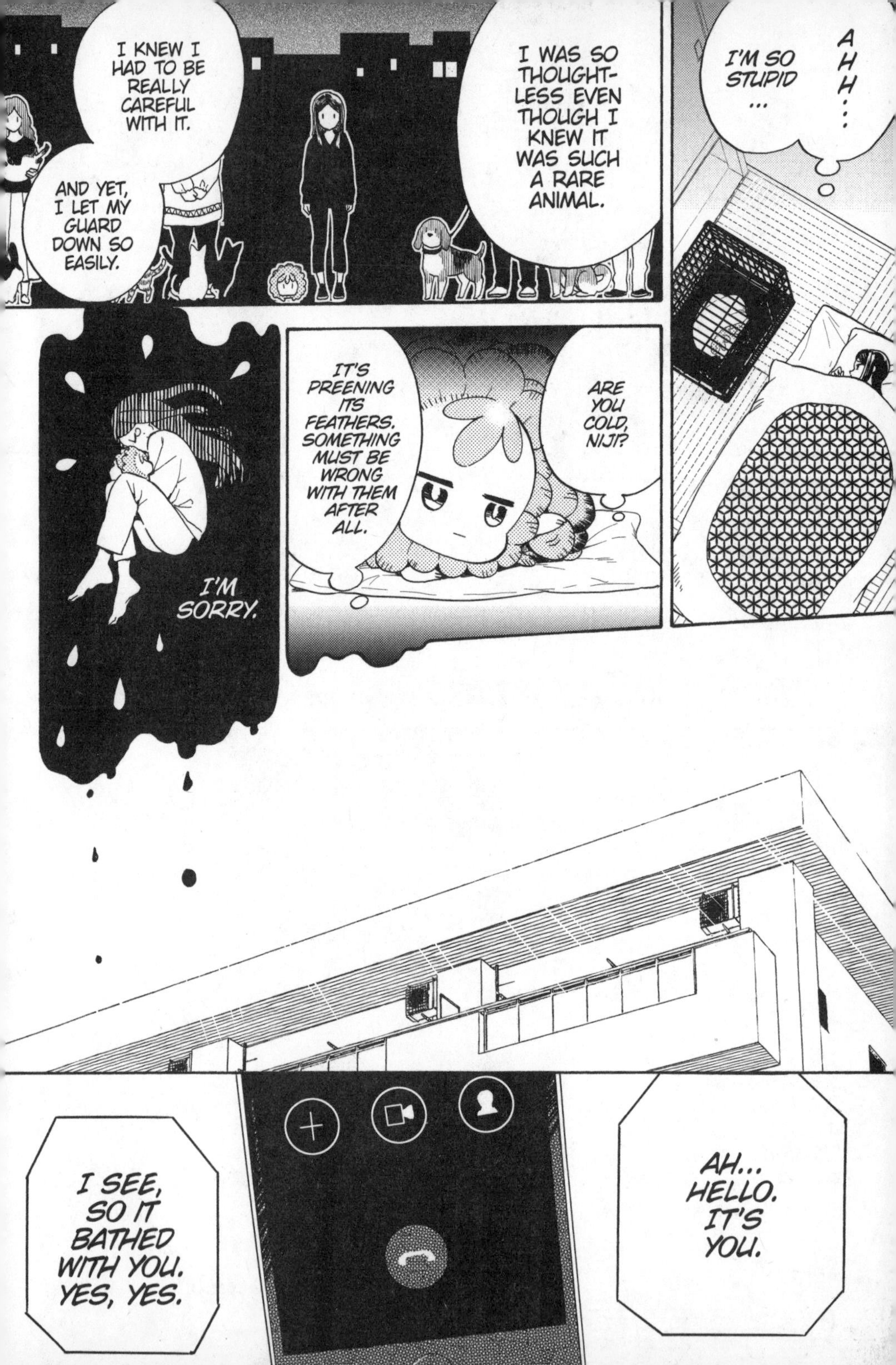
AHH...
I'M SO STUPID ...
I WAS SO THOUGHT-LESS EVEN THOUGH I KNEW IT WAS SUCH A RARE ANIMAL.
I KNEW I HAD TO BE REALLY CAREFUL WITH IT.
AND YET, I LET MY GUARD DOWN SO EASILY.
ARE YOU COLD, NIJI?
IT'S PREENING ITS FEATHERS. SOMETHING MUST BE WRONG WITH THEM AFTER ALL.
I'M SORRY.
AH... HELLO. IT'S YOU.
I SEE, SO IT BATHED WITH YOU. YES, YES.

I'M SURE NIJI-KUN JUST WANTED TO TAKE A BATH...

WITH YOU.

NO... *UM,* WHAT I MEAN IS!

I ACCI-DENTALLY BATHED HIM IN HOT WATER.

WE'RE TAKING HIM TO THE HOSPITAL NOW.

NO NEED.

HAPPY MICE OWNERS OFTEN LET THEM BATHE IN HOT SPRINGS.

THEY'RE A BIT LIKE JAPANESE MONKEYS.

THEY HAVE NO PROBLEMS BATHING IN WARM WATER.

YOUR RESEARCH WAS RIGHT.
THE OIL ON BIRD FEATHERS ACTS AS A WATER REPELLANT.

MOST BIRDS HAVE A **UROPYGIAL GLAND** THAT SECRETES OIL NEAR THEIR HIP.
THEY SPREAD THAT OIL ONTO THEIR FEATHERS AS THEY PREEN.

BUT THE MELTING POINT FOR THAT OIL IS HIGHER THAN NORMAL ON A HAPPY MOUSE.
THE GLANDS SECRETE THE OIL DIFFER-ENTLY AS WELL.

THEY BATHE THAT WAY IN THE WILD, TOO.
IN NATURAL HOT SPRINGS.
FLOP...

WE CALL THIS THE HAPPY SEBACEOUS GLAND.
"HAPPY SEBA-CEOUS GLAND"?

THEY'RE FINE IN WATER AT FORTY-TWO DEGREES CELSIUS.
THEIR GLANDS SECRETE MORE OIL RIGHT AFTER A WARM BATH, SO THEY TEND TO PREEN EACH OTHER'S FEATHERS TO SPREAD IT FASTER.

THEY ALSO RELEASE A VERY CAPTIVATING FRAGRANCE.
?!
HAVE YOU NOTICED IT?
I DIDN'T NOTICE BEFORE BECAUSE I WAS SO DEPRESSED...
BUT I CAN SMELL A FAINT FRUITY SCENT FROM THE KITCHEN.
YES.
YES! IT DOES HAVE A VERY CAPTIVATING FRA-GRANCE!

THERE ARE MANY BIRDS FROM PREDATOR-LIGHT ENVIRONMENTS IN THE SOUTHERN HEMISPHERE THAT EMIT SIMILAR SCENTS FROM THEIR BODY.
MOM, HE SAID IT'S OKAY FOR IT TO BATHE IN WARM WATER.
HUH?! WHY?!
AMONG THEM, THE RAINBOW-COLORED HEAVENLY PARROT HAS ONE OF THE BEST FRAGRANCES.
JUST ANOTHER REASON WHY THEY'RE SO POPULAR.
IF SOMEONE ASKED ME WHAT THE BIG DEAL WAS ABOUT IT EMITTING A FRA-GRANCE ...
I'D SAY THAT IT'S NOT REALLY A BIG DEAL AT ALL.
YOU REALLY ARE ONE CRAZY ANIMAL.
THRILL...

SNIFF

HEY, MOM.

WHAT WOULD YOU SAY THIS FRAGRANCE IS?

VANILLA... FLOWERS...

POP-CORN...

WHEAT ...?

LAVENDER OIL AFTER TWO DAYS...?

OH MY.
YAWN...
WELL, SHE DIDN'T SLEEP WELL LAST NIGHT.

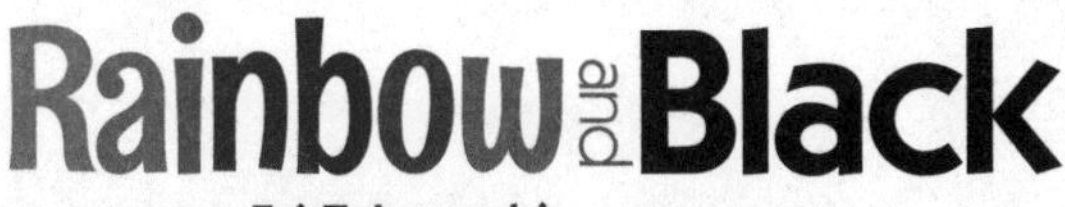
Rainbow and Black
Story & Art by Eri Takenashi

NOW LOADING...

BRING
ING
ING
ING
ING
ING
ING
RATTLE
NIJI.
GOOD MORNING.

GOOD MORNING.
YES. GOOD MORNING.
GOOD MORNING!!
GOOD MORNING!
GOOD MORNING.

#3 Cries

ぶわっ
BWUFFLE
PLOOP
POOP.
RUFFLE RUFFLE
WOW! YOU DID SUCH A GREAT JOB! YOU POOPED!
YOU MADE POOP!
POOP!
POOP!
POOP!
♪ ♪
POOP—♪

POO...

KURO!
WHAT?
KURO!
KURO!
KURO...
KURO!
KU--
KURO!
KURO!
KURO!
HA...
KU
RO
SNRK!
KU!
RO!
KU!
WHAT?!
SCRATCH SCRATCH...

GOOD MORNING.

GOOD MORNING-!

RICE FOR BREAKFAST? OR BREAD?

BREAD.

HERE.

BREAKFAST, NIJI.

THANK YOU FOR THE FOOD.

THANK YOU FOR THE FOOD.

THAN-AN-AN-AN-ANK YOU FOR THE FOOD.

WHAT'S YOUR SCHEDULE TODAY?
I HAVE A LECTURE DURING SECOND PERIOD.
THEN I'VE GOT MY NEW PART-TIME JOB, SO I WON'T BE HOME UNTIL NIGHT.
WHAT ABOUT YOU, MOM?
WORKING FROM HOME TODAY.
I'M OFF.
HAVE A GOOD DAY.
HAVE A GOOD DAY.

I'M HOME!
WELCOME HOME!
OH, WELCOME HOME...
HUH ?!
IT JUST SAID, "WELCOME HOME!" ON ITS OWN?!

IT MUST HAVE MEMORIZED THE WORDS.

JUST LIKE YOU SAID.
AT THIS RATE, CAN IT HAVE CONVER-SATIONS WITH US?

CONVER-SATIONS, HUH...?
WHO KNOWS?

TO BE HONEST ...

PET OWNERS OFTEN SAY THAT.
"MY OO-CHAN CAN SPEAK~!"
I NEVER CARED FOR IT.

ISN'T THAT JUST A FANTASY THAT ALL PET LOVERS WISH FOR?
YEAH... WELL...

EVEN AFTER IT'S BEEN SCIEN-TIFICALLY PROVEN THAT PETS AREN'T CAPABLE OF HUMAN LANGUAGE.

NIJI TELLS ME "POOP"...
BUT ALWAYS AFTER THE FACT, RIGHT?
IT'S JUST MIMICKING THE WORDS THAT HUMANS SAY.
AND I REINFORCE THAT BY COMPLIMENTING IT...
WHICH IS WHY IT SAYS THE WORD EVEN WHEN IT DIDN'T ACTUALLY POOP.
MOM... IT'S NOT A "CONVER-SATION."
FOR
WHAT
FISH
IT'S JUST A "CUE" FOR THEM.
HUMANS ARE HUMANS! ANIMALS ARE ANIMALS!
BLACK AND WHITE.
I DON'T THINK IT'S GOOD TO CONFUSE THE TWO!
CLEARLY

WE SHOULD JUST HAVE FUN WITH IT!
WHAT DO YOU MEAN?
ARE WE STILL ON THE SAME SUBJECT?
IT'S FINE! JUST HAVE FUN!
IT'S NOT FINE!!
THAT'S NOT WHAT I MEANT...
HMMPH!
THE BATHING FIASCO HAPPENED BECAUSE WE TREATED IT TOO MUCH LIKE A HUMAN!
I DON'T WANT TO MAKE A MISTAKE LIKE THAT EVER AGAIN!
THAT'S CARELESS THINKING!

BRING
ING
ING
ING
ING
GASP!

KURO, WHAT ABOUT BREAKFAST?
I DON'T HAVE TIME. EAT WITHOUT ME!
I OVERSLEPT!

BA-TONK...

CHIRP
CHIRP

BZZZZ

Mom
This is bad! Niji just keeps crying "Kuro Kuro."
10:20
It's been looking for you all day.
It won't stop crying.🤣🤣🤣

won't stop crying.🤣🤣🤣
In class right n
I can't stand this racket.💢💢
Aa

een looking for y
won't stop crying.🤣🤣🤣
10:20
(read)
10:22
I can't stand this racket.💢💢
10:22
Call me after your class. Let it hear your voice.😅

JEEZ, MOM!
WILL YOU STOP CONTACTING ME FOR SUCH LITTLE THINGS?
IT'S NOT A "LITTLE THING" AT ALL!
KURO!
IT REALLY WON'T STOP CRYING!
KURO!
IT ALWAYS CRIES OUT MY NAME LIKE THAT.
I'M SWITCHING TO VIDEO CHAT!
HUH?! WAIT!
WE DON'T HAVE TO GO THAT FAR!
MOM ?!
RUFFLE RUSTLE
SEE, NIJI-CHAN?
LOOK, IT'S KURO!
KURO.
KURO IS OUT-SIDE!
CAN YOU SEE HER?
HEY. SAY SOMETHING, KURO.
WILL YOU LET IT HEAR YOUR VOICE?
IT'S STARING SO IN-TENTLY.
UM...
HI, NIJI.
I'M HERE.

HAVE A GOOD DAY!

It's quiet now.
10 : 39

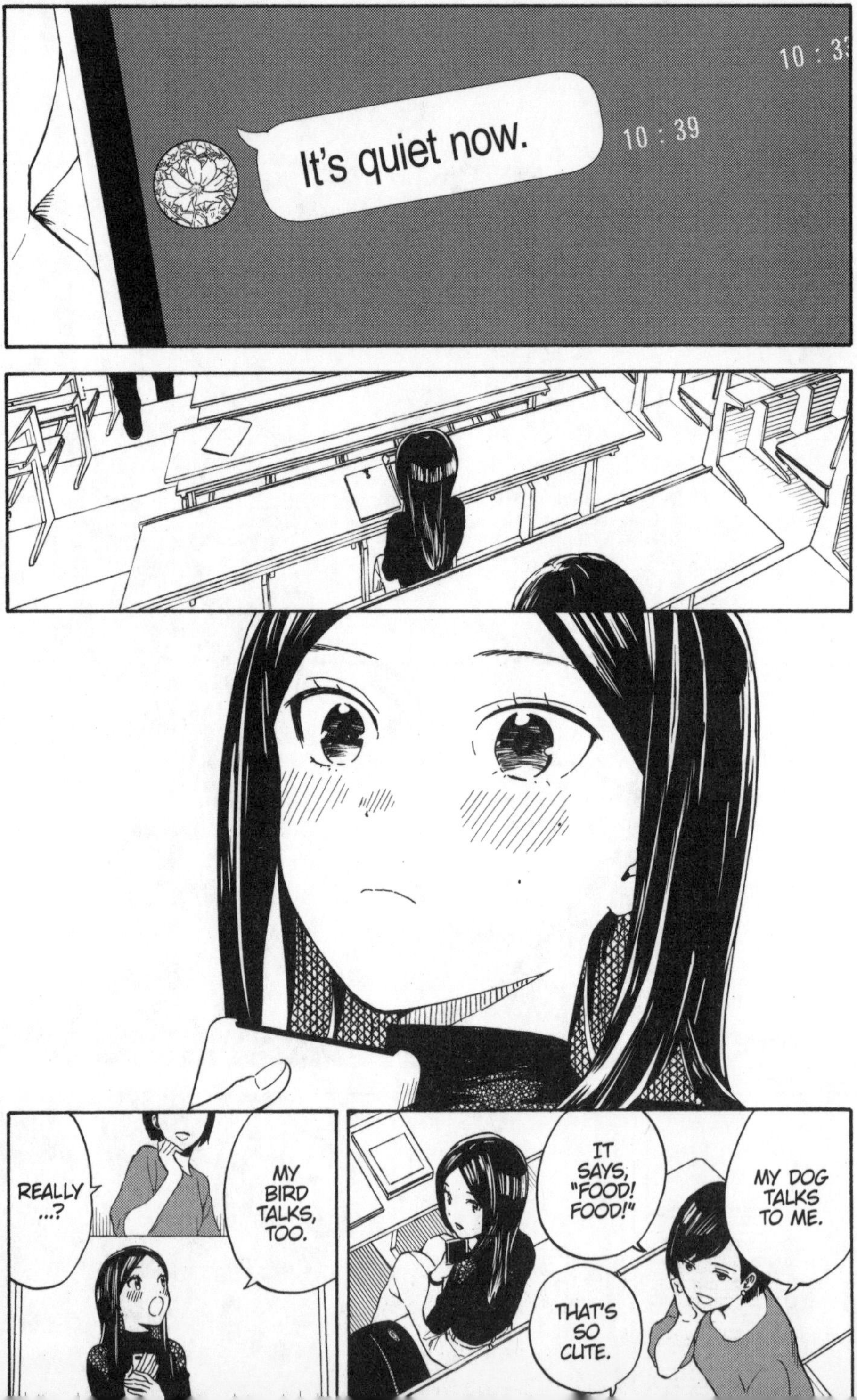

MY DOG TALKS TO ME.
IT SAYS, "FOOD! FOOD!"
THAT'S SO CUTE.
MY BIRD TALKS, TOO.
REALLY ...?

Rainbow and Black
Story & Art by Eri Takenashi

NOW LOADING...

#4 Courtship Behavior

CAN YOU HOLD A CONVER-SATION?

JUST HOW MUCH...

DO YOU...

HOUSE SMILE NIJI-CHAN GYOKIN, RIGHT?
NOT! REALLY!
THAT WASN'T GOOD AT ALL.
THAT WASN'T A CONVERSATION.
POOP. NOT REALLY!
NIJI-CHAN, YOU SHOULD STOP THAT...
HMM...
POOP. NIJI-CHAN SUCH A GOOD JOB! NOT REALLY! AT! ALL!

KURO!
WHAT?
KURO!
WHAT?
KURO!
WHAT?
ROLL
ROLL
ROLL
KURO!
WHAT?
KURO.
WHAT?
NIJI!
WHAT?

WHOA...
THIS. THIS IS IT ...!

NIJI.
WHAT?

CRACK
CRACK
SHATTER
I CAN'T TELL WHAT'S BLACK AND WHAT'S WHITE!

DIDN'T YOU KNOW?

I-I KNEW THAT!

BUT WE CAN COMMUNICATE...

MORE THAN I THOUGHT.

HEGERU, RIGHT!

IT SEEMS TO UNDERSTAND SIMPLE VOCABULARY.
MEATLESS NOODLES, RIGHT!
DON'T THEY SAY THAT DOGS AND CATS HAVE THE INTELLIGENCE OF A TODDLER?
MAYBE BIRDS HAVE A HIGHER INTELLIGENCE.
MA YU NE.

IT'S CUTE, LIKE HAVING A LITTLE KID LIVING WITH US.
RIGHT?!
NIJI-CHAN IS CUTE!
CUTE!
CUTE!
NIJI-CHAN IS CUTE!
NIJI-CHAN IS CUTE!
NUZZLE NUZZLE
NIJI-CHAN IS CUTE!
LOOKS LIKE IT UNDERSTANDS THE WORD "CUTE."
YUP.
KURO...
IS CUTE.

KURO IS CUTE.
KURO !!!S CUTE!
CUTE! CUTE!
KURO CU KURO CU KURO.
KURO...
IS CUTE.
HUP...
THIS...
IS IT SAYING THAT BECAUSE IT KNOWS WHAT IT MEANS?
.....
PROBA-BLY?
WELL, BUT THAT WAS MULTIPLE WORDS.
AND THE SENTENCE WAS PROPERLY PARSED.

YOU'RE CUTE.
NIJI IS CUTE.
BUJURU DEGYURU BOGYA DYURU-RURU GYUDYUBE JURURU.
WHOA.
HOP
HOP
HOP
HOP
HOP
HOP
HOP
THAT FLIPPED A SWITCH.
IT REALLY LIKES YOU.
I'M JEALOUS!
Hop
Hop
Hop
ARE YOU SERIOUS?
HUFF! HUFF!
SHWP...
DID IT CALM DOWN?

HEY.
CALL ME CUTE, TOO.
"RIE-SAN IS CUTE."
"RIE-SAN IS CUTE."
COME ON.

KURO IS CUTE.
KURO IS CUTE.
KURO IS CUTE.

KURO...
HAA! HAA!
IS CUTE...

KUUURO...
IS CUUUTE.

KURO IS CUTE...
MOOOOOM!
IS... IS IT REALLY ...
ALL RIGHT FOR ME TO BE BATHING WITH HIM LIKE THIS?!
IT DOESN'T FEEL LIKE BATHING WITH A SMALL CHILD...
MORE LIKE... WELL...
RIGHT! IT'S LIKE A GUY...
WHO WANTS TO BE WITH ME OR SOME-THING!

BE WITH YOU ...?
WELL, THAT MAKES SENSE.
HE'S YOUR BOY-FRIEND, AFTER ALL.
HE'S YOUR PARTNER, RIGHT?
YOU CAN NEVER BE SEPA-RATED.
NOT UNTIL HE FINISHES HIS EIGHTY YEARS OF LIFE.
NO WAY!
I DON'T EVEN HAVE A HUMAN BOYFRIEND YET!
STILL, THOUGH...

KURO IS CUTE.
STRONG ARMS...
KURO... IS CUTE...
KURO... IS CUTE...
DEEP VOICE...
IT'S A MAN...
KURO... IS CUTE...

KURO...
IS CUTE...

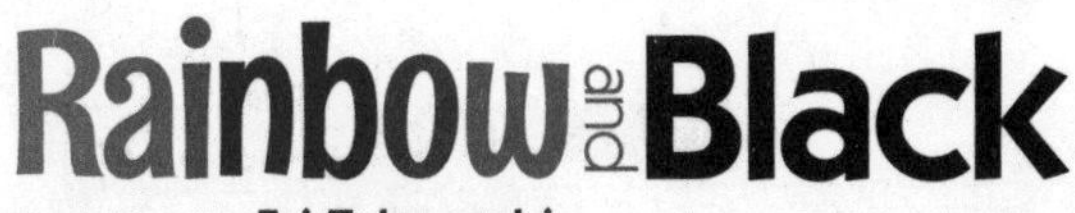
Rainbow and Black
Story & Art by Eri Takenashi

NOW LOADING...

#5 Playing with Food

I QUIT MY JOB.
YOU GOT FIRED AGAIN?!
AGAIN ?!
AGAIN ?!
WHAT WAS THE REASON THIS TIME?!
STOP SAYING "AGAIN" OVER AND OVER...

This is a customer appreciation fair...

so you should properly appreciate your customers!

During an exchange of goods...

the customer and the seller have equal standing.

A "customer appreciation fair"...

is a day when we give thanks to all the customers who support us.

That is what I believe.

Oh, I see!
Is that the policy of this store?
That's what your superiors say?
No.
This is my personal opinion.

SO TROUBLE-SOME.

RIGHT? IT WAS *REALLY* TROUBLE-SOME.

WHY DID SHE--

I'M NOT TALKING ABOUT *HER.*

I MEAN YOU.

?

WHY DIDN'T YOU LEAVE IT TO THE MANAGER?

IT'S NOT YOUR JOB TO DEAL WITH THINGS LIKE THAT.

THE MANAGEMENT CAN'T SAY ANYTHING BECAUSE OF THEIR POSITIONS!

BUT I'M JUST A PART-TIME WORKER.

THINGS CAN BE RESOLVED AS LONG AS I QUIT.

STUPID!

MANAGE-MENT NOW HAS MORE WORK BECAUSE OF YOU!
A PERSON WHO COMPLAINS LIKE THAT WON'T BACK OFF SO EASILY.
THEY'LL HAVE TO APOLOGIZE TO HER.
ON TOP OF THAT, THEY NEED TO HIRE A NEW PART-TIME WORKER!

YOU CAUSED TROUBLE...
FOR THEM, TOO!

WHAT DOES IT MEAN TO HAVE A JOB...?

LOOKS LIKE I DID SOMETHING THAT WASN'T PART OF MY JOB...
THAT PERSON SAID, "I'M NOT REALLY COMPLAINING"...
AS SHE WAS ORDERING AROUND THE VARIOUS STAFF.
PTOO
BE-SHUK

"I'M DOING THEM A FAVOR," SHE SAID.

DOESN'T THAT MEAN SHE DIDN'T UNDERSTAND HER OWN ACTIONS?

THAT'S WHY I DIDN'T THINK SHE WAS REALLY...

A BAD PERSON, YOU KNOW.

BE-SHUK

IF I EXPLAINED PROPERLY...

I THOUGHT THAT MAYBE SHE WOULD UNDERSTAND.

KONK

I THOUGHT YOU UNDER-STOOD WHEN I TALKED TO YOU.
HEY! LISTEN TO ME!

OHYOU!!
GA-THUD

WHAT KIND OF WORD IS "OHYOU"?
THAT'S A NEW ONE.

WHAT IS...
THAT?
TOK
TOK
TOK
TOK TOK
TOK

NIJI-CHAN IS...

CUTE!

ARE YOU...

DRESSING UP?

HUFF! HUFF!
TUMBLE
TUMBLE
I'M STARTING...
TO NOT CARE ANYMORE.
A JOB.
WHAT'S IN A JOB, ANYWAY?

YOU'RE AMAZING.
BO-YOING

NIJI IS AMAZING.
NIJI IS AMAZING.
AH HA HA! HE ALREADY MEMORIZED THAT.
NIJI IS AMAZING.
THAT'S RIGHT. AMAZING!
NOO... NOT REEEALLY.
MAU MAU...
"MAU MAU."
?
HE SAID THAT BEFORE.
WHAT DOES IT MEAN?

Rainbow and Black
Story & Art by Eri Takenashi

NOW LOADING...

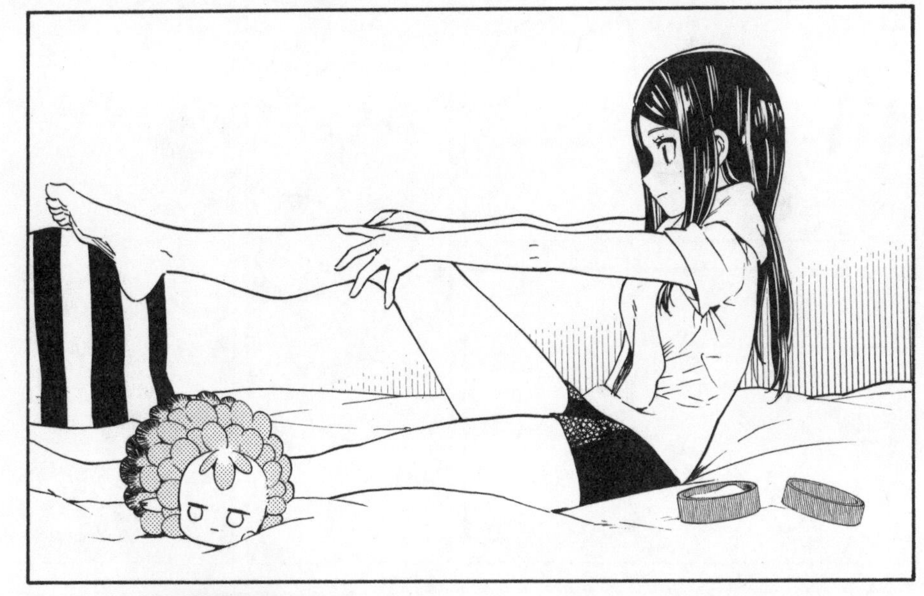

WHEW...

YOU SMELL SO GOOD AFTER A BATH, NIJI.

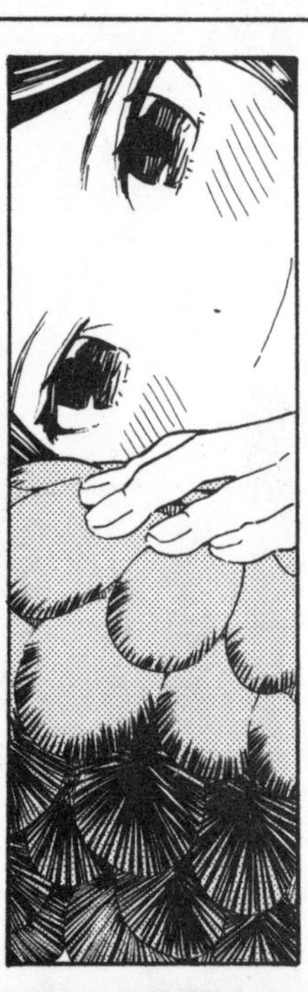

OH.

HE SAID IT AGAIN.

#6 Biology

GYA——!!

GATHER! EXOTIC SPECIES OF THE WORLD

YOU WANTED ME TO SEE A VERREAUX'S SIFAKA?

THAT'S NOT IT. AFTER THIS. IT'S COMING UP NEXT.

GATHER! EXOTIC SPECIES OF THE WORLD

Welcome to "Gather! Exotic Species of the World"!

GIANT PANDA

GALAPAGOS KOMODO DRAGON

On this show, we bring you information about different exotic species each week.

This week, we'd like to explore the biology of the rainbow-colored heavenly parrot.
OH HO!
RAINBOW-COLORED HEAVENLY PARROT

AH...
THIS...
THIS IS...
RIGHT? THAT'S WHY I YELPED.

WE HAVE TO WATCH THIS. WE *HAVE* TO.
SIT UP STRAIGHT.

A certain island in the South Pacific...
Hohetsuhekkyorurihoho Island.
HOHE--WHAT? HUH?
HOHETSUHEKKYORURIHOHO ISLAND.

It's home to a unique species called the rainbow-colored heavenly parrot.

WHOA-HO!

This individual is currently mimicking a frog.
GUU-WUH... GUU-WUH...
GUU-WUH... GUU-WUH...
They excel at voice mimicry and add all sorts of sounds to their repertoire.
YES. THAT MAKES SENSE.
SO, THEY'RE MORE SKILLED THAN A NORMAL BIRD.
Now, they have the word "parrot" in their name...
but they are not actually birds.
I KNEW THAT.
They have no beaks or wings.
The first people to discover the species thought they were a kind of squirrel or mouse.
OHHH. THAT'S WHY PEOPLE CALL THEM "HAPPY MICE"...
However, scientists currently believe that they are a completely different species with their own unique branch of evolution.
Now, let's look at their biology.
These are rainbow-colored heavenly parrot eggs.
THEY AREN'T EVEN TRYING TO HIDE THE EGGS.
LOOK HOW COLOR-FUL THEY ARE.

The mother and father take turns warming the eggs.

Look!
They're hatching!
These are rainbow-colored heavenly parrot babies!

As soon as they are born, they grab onto their mother's stomach.
Now they're drinking from their mother's nipples.
THE MOTHER LACTATES EVEN THOUGH SHE LAID EGGS?!
I KNEW THAT.

HUH? YOU KNEW THAT?
I READ IT ON ITS WIKI PAGE.
Neither bird nor mammal, its evolution is still under much debate by scientists.
I WONDER... IF IT'S PART OF THE PLATYPUS FAMILY.
IF SCIENTISTS SAY IT'S A MYSTERY, IT'S PROBABLY A MYSTERY.

Why did they undergo such a unique evolution?
It's believed that the secret was their environment.
Hohetsuhekkyorurihoho Island is completely isolated.
HOHE--WHAT?
In the middle is a mountain that juts up vertically as if it were cut out.
A cluster of trees grows in the forest at the top of this mountain.
The forest is their home.
It is a tree unique to this island...
the eroero tree.
THE NAME!
THAT NAME! THAT NAME IS--!

This tree is actually highly poisonous.
HUH ?!
How can these creatures live safely in such dangerous trees?
It is believed that they are able to neutralize the poison inside their bodies.
However, the truth is uncertain.
By living in a forest of eroero trees, the rainbow-colored heavenly parrots protect themselves from any predators.
A FOREST OF EROERO TREES.
THAT JUST SOUNDS ...
They clearly have evolved in their own unique way.
What's this...?
The entire colony is on the move.
Where are they planning to go?

It looks like they've arrived at a spring.
Steam is rising up from its surface.
These creatures have come to soak in the hot springs!
OH... AHA!
TH... THAT'S IT! THAT'S IT!
THIS IS WHY--!
THIS IS WHY--!
They have begun grooming each other.
Their behavior is like that of Japanese monkeys.
They reinforce their bonds with one another as they do so.

This cry... Do you know what kind of cry this is?
MAU MAU.
This cry is often heard in the middle of grooming or when someone in their colony shares food with them.
MAU MAU.
MAU MAU.
We had a zoologist study this strange cry that they make during such social interac-tion.

They don't make this cry with humans that they see only when they bring food.
They do not make that cry when an automated dispenser gives them food.
08:00
MAU MAU.
DO YOU WANT SOME, TOO?
However, if they form a bond with a human and accept them as part of their family...
they will begin to make this cry.

In other words...
they only make this cry to creatures in their community with whom they have established a mutual relationship of support.
Also...
Individuals that make this "mau mau" cry often...
MAU MAU.
MAU MAU.
are much more com-municative within their colony.
Scientists believe that this cry...
is like the words "thank you" among humans.

Giving an obvious sign of "thanks."
Rainbow-colored heavenly parrots are the only non-human species confirmed to do this.
We believe...
this proves that the social structure of rainbow-colored heavenly parrots is built upon an advanced level of communication.
The rainbow-colored heavenly parrot is a strange yet loving creature that highly treasures the bonds built within its colony.
Their society may be quite similar to that of humans.

WHAT'S WRONG?
NOTHING... IT'S JUST...
I FEEL A BIT MOVED.

Rainbow and Black
Story & Art by Eri Takenashi

NOW LOADING...

¥999
#7 Looking for Friends

YOU KNOW, HIRO-KUUUN... HE TOLD ME HE WANTED TO GO TO THE HOT SPRINGS.
AND THEN HE SAID THAT EVEN IF IT WEREN'T A HOT SPRING, HE'D BE OKAY STAYING OVERNIGHT ANYWHERE.
REALLY, THAT'S ALL MEN EVER THINK ABOUT!
RIGHT? ISN'T THAT PRETTY CRAZY?
DESPERATION IS SUCH A TURNOFF, RIGHT?
IT JUST MAKES ME CRINGE!
YOU SHOULD MAKE ANOTHER BOYFRIEND.
I BROKE UP WITH MY LAST ONE OVER THE SAME THING.
YUUKA, DIDN'T YOU GO TO THE HOT SPRINGS WITH YOUR BOYFRIEND LAST TIME?
THAT WASN'T MY BOYFRIEND-- IT WAS AN UPPER-CLASSMAN.
HUH? OH, NO.
NO WAY. REALLY? THAT'S CRAZY.

WHAT ABOUT YOU, SHIRAHOSHI-SAN?
AREN'T YOU GOING TO MAKE A BOYFRIEND?

HUH?!
I THINK YOU FIND A BOYFRIEND, NOT MAKE ONE...
BUT IF I JUST BLURT THAT OUT, IT'LL CAUSE PROBLEMS, RIGHT?
I'M NOT... I DON'T REALLY...

I'M PRETTY BUSY.

BY THE WAY!

I WENT TO MOZY RECENTLY!

I ONLY GO TO THE SHIBUYA OR SHIMOKITA SHOPS.

I GET YOU! THOSE TWO ARE REALLY FANCY!

SHIRAHOSHI-SAN...
WHICH MOZY SHOP DO YOU LIKE BEST?

HUH ?!
ISN'T THIS QUESTION BASED ON THE ASSUMPTION THAT I LIKE THAT SHOP AT ALL?!

IT'S A SWEETS CAFÉ THAT'S CURRENTLY POPULAR, RIGHT...?
I WASN'T REALLY INTERESTED IN IT, SO I DON'T KNOW ANYTHING ABOUT IT.
BUT I CAN'T JUST SAY I DON'T KNOW ABOUT IT IN THIS SITUATION...
WELL... UM...
THAT'S...

I'VE HEARD OF IT EFORE, UT...

LET'S GO TOMORROW!

I HEARD YOU CAN GET CREDIT FOR THE CLASS EVEN IF YOU ONLY SHOW UP ONCE!

WE DON'T REALLY NEED TO ATTEND THAT CLASS, ANYWAY.

I WISH *ALL* OUR CLASSES WERE LIKE THAT!

WELCOME HOME.
I'M HOME.
HOW WAS SCHOOL?
ARE YOU GETTING ALONG WITH YOUR FRIENDS?
YEAH!

I WANTED ...
TO TALK ABOUT HOW INTERESTING THE CLASS WAS.
OR HOW THANKFUL I AM TO MY PARENTS FOR LETTING ME GO TO COLLEGE.
THAT'S THE KIND OF CONVERSATION I WANTED.
THEY OPENLY IGNORED ME BECAUSE I DIDN'T KNOW WHAT THEY WERE TALKING ABOUT...
I WOULD NEVER DO SOMETHING LIKE THAT, SO I JUST DON'T UNDER-STAND.
IS THIS JUST WHAT COLLEGE IS LIKE?
IT'S NOT REALLY DIFFERENT FROM THE CLAUSTRO-PHOBIC CLASSES IN HIGH SCHOOL.
MOST OF THE HUMAN RELATIONSHIPS IN CLASS HAVE ALREADY BEEN FORMED.
IT'D BE HARD TO MAKE FRIENDS WITH ANOTHER GROUP NOW.

HOW DID THIS HAPPEN?
I MADE A FEW FRIENDS DURING THE FLOWER VIEWING FESTIVAL FOR NEW STUDENTS.
BUT THE GIRLS I THOUGHT I'D GET ALONG WITH HAD A DIFFERENT MAJOR...
AND THE ONES IN MY MAJOR ARE ALL LIKE THOSE TWO GIRLS TODAY.
....
....
I TOTALLY FAILED AT MAKING FRIENDS
BEING ALONE.
BEING ALONE SUCKS...

HM?
Recommended User
Nana
@nanachan0521
FOLLOW
I am the happy mouse Nana-chan.
Entertainment News
Comedy/Variety
1 hr ago
A RAINBOW-COLORED HEAVENLY PARROT...
ICON.

Nana @nanachan0521

FOLLOW

56 Followers — 20 Follows —

There are no other followers

IT DOESN'T HAVE A LOT OF FOLLOW-ERS...

NO... THAT'S NORMAL UNLESS YOU'RE FAMOUS OR SOME-THING.

HOW LONG HAS THIS ACCOUNT BEEN ACTIVE?
A FEW MONTHS... IT SEEMS?
Nana
Favorite
WHO IS THE USER CONNECTED TO?
LOOKS LIKE THEY'RE MOSTLY PET LOVERS ...
THE USER'S REAL FRIENDS?
Niboshi Cat's House
@oas9v51s22v
Think Care
@oijgfspkr
IN... IN THE MUTUAL FOLLOW LIST!
THERE'S ANOTHER OWNER!
Larc
@larc_san
Rainbow-colored
Feel free to follow
THERE'S... ANOTHER ONE.
THEY'RE CONNECTED.
THA-THUMP
DO THEY TALK TO EACH OTHER?
DO THEY MEET EACH OTHER IN PERSON?
I SHOULD LOOK AT THE REPLIES.
WHAT KIND OF CONVERSATIONS HAVE THEY BEEN HAVING?
OH, MAN. I'M LIKE AN INTERNET STALKER.

COMPARED TO "NANA"-SAN...
Nana @nanachan0521
Nana-chan has gotten ch
How do you train a happy
1
NANA
@nanachan0521
BUT I DID FIND THREE REPLIES.
"LARC"-SAN DOESN'T TWEET MUCH.
Larc @larc_san
Replying @nanachan0521
Its behavior is cute compared to my little princess.
1
LARC
@larc_san
THEY ALSO DM EACH OTHER SO THEY MUST BE CLOSE. MAYBE THEY'RE REAL-LIFE FRIENDS?
Nana @nanachan0521
Replying larc_san
Is it okay to DM you?
Nana
Replying larc_san
Larc-chan is a aquatic plant junkie
1
Nana @nanachan0521
Replying @nanachan0521
I wonder why she is so obsessed with them...
SO... JEALOUS...
SO, OWNERS HAVE CONVERSATIONS LIKE THIS WITH EACH OTHER.
Nana @nanachan0521
I went to Seibu-Shinjuku's 100 y
shop popo.
Nana @nanachan0521
The Chuou Line has stopped.
SHE LIVES IN TOKYO...
Houji Tea Latte
HAVEN'T I SEEN THIS STARBOCKS BEFORE...?

OUR DAILY COMMON SPACES...
OVERLAP.
THA-THUMP

WHAT SHOULD I DO?
THA-THUMP
THA-THUMP
I'M GETTING SUPER HOPEFUL.

IF IT'S JUST FOLLOWING...
I WONDER IF IT'S OKAY...?
I ONLY FOLLOW THE NEWS AND INFORMATION ON EARTH-QUAKES ON MY ACCOUNT.
Indianacrow @
5 Follows 0 Followers
I JUST LOOK LIKE A PASSER-BY.
han0521
Follow
an.
TAP!
PHEW!
TH...
THAT STARTLED ME...!
PA-PING

★ Try sending a reply to someone.
Nana @nanachan0521
Replying @indianacrow
Thank you for following me!
HUH ?!
SHE RESPONDED SO FAST!
WHAT SHOULD I DO...?
I WAS JUST PLANNING ON LOOKING AT HER POSTS...
Indianacrow @Indianacrow
Replying @nanachan0521
Thank you for letting me follow you.
I look forward to your posts.
I REPLIED TO HER.
IT'S FINE, RIGHT?
I'M JUST BEING POLITE.
SHE HAS LOTS OF OTHER FOLLOWERS BESIDES ME.

Nana gets on top of me and I can't get any work done!
Nana @nanachan0521
I've been working on making something and Nana keeps looking at me with "That's for me, right?" eyes...
No, it's not yours...
Don't think that everything humans make is always for you.
Nana @nanachan0521
Thank goodness she ate her new food!
Larc @larc_san
I am being dragged around by larc-san today, too.
What a reward.
Nana @nanachan0521
The whole world must see just how cute the butthole of a happy mouse is.
Nana @nanachan0521
Mysterious sleeping position.

Larc @larc_san
Feeling that larc-sama's love
has gotten too heavy.
Never.

   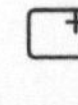

Nana @nanachan0521
[Today's Nana-chan]
She only eats the color red

Larc @larc_san
Weight is now 3.1kg
Princess Larc has
gained weight.
Time for a diet?

Nana @nanachan0521
Nana-chan fights with
a CD-R.

Nana @nanachan0521
I heard that there is a happy mouse
run for happy mice overseas.

Nana @nanachan0521
How many people own a happy mouse in
the greater Tokyo area?
Tell me if you own one~~~

   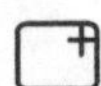

#wantstoconnectwithhappymouseowners

Monday
Tuesday
HAA!
HAA!

#wantstoconnectwithhappymouseowners

1

Indianacrow @Indianacrow 10 sec

I also own one!

You have a new tweet ↑

1 2

Nana @nanachan0521 3 sec

Replying : @indianacrow

UWOOOOOOOOOOOOOOOOOOOOOOOOOO
OOOOOOOOOOOOOOOOOOOOOOOOOOOO
OOOOOOOOOOOOOOOOOOOOOOOOOOOO
OOOOO!!!!!!!!!!!!!!!!!!!!!!!!!!!!!!!

3 2

Nana @nanachan0521 1 sec
Replying : @indianacrow
UWOOOOOOOOOOOOOOOOOOOOOO
OOOOOOOOOOOOOOOOOOOOOOOO
OOOOOOOOOOOOOOOOOOOOOOOO
OOOOO!!!!!!!!!!!!!!!!!!!!!!!!!!

1

Larc @larc_san 1 sec
Replying: @nanachan @Indianacroww
We finally fend one.

1

Larc @larc_san 30 sec
Replying: @larc_san @nanachan0521
Correction. We finally found one.

1

Nana @nanachan0521 15 sec
Replying: @Indianacrow
You live in Japan, don't you?!?

Rainbow and Black
Story & Art by Eri Takenashi

NOW LOADING...

Nana @nanachan0521
Let's play with nail clippers.
LIKE!
Indianacrow @Indianacrow
7 Follows — 2 Followers —
★You do not have any tweets.

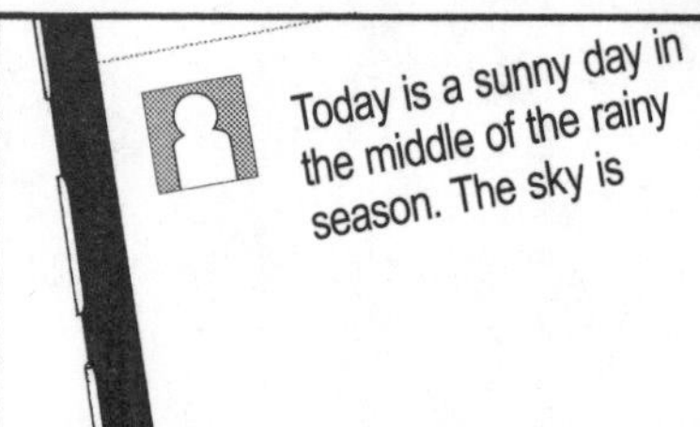
Today is a sunny day in the middle of the rainy season. The sky is

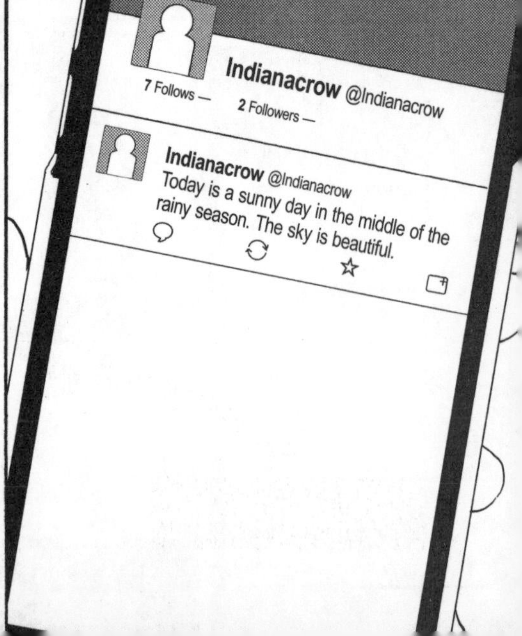
Indianacrow @Indianacrow
7 Follows —
2 Followers —
Indianacrow @Indianacrow
Today is a sunny day in the middle of the rainy season. The sky is beautiful.

#8 Chirping

Indianacrow @Indianacrow
Today is a sunny day in the middle of the rainy season. The sky is beautiful.
1
1
Nana @nanachan0521
Replying: @Indianacrow
It feels so great today~♪
PA-PING★
NANA-CHAN AND HER OWNER ARE LOOKING AT THIS SAME SKY.
THE SKY IS SO BEAUTIFUL.

WHOA!
THE SKYYY IS SO BEAUTIFUL. SO CUTE.
H-HE SANG ...!
HE JUST SANG. RIGHT?
I KNEW THEY SANG...
BUT TO THINK THAT YOU'D SING ABOUT THE BEAUTIFUL SKY. WHAT A WONDERFUL CREATURE YOU ARE.

I SEE...

Indianacrow @Indianacrow
Niji just sang.
He sang, "The sky is so beautiful.
So cute."
So cute."
1
Nana @nanachan0521
Replying: @Indianacrow
Wow! That'd be nice to hear!
Mine sings when she's in a good mood, too~!

Indianacrow @Indianacrow
Replying: @nanachan0521
Do you think he's in a good mood?
It surprised me because it's the first time
I've heard him sing.
1
Nana @nanachan0521
Replying: @Indianacrow
Maybe Niji-chan is still in the process of learning words?
I hear that males tend to sing more often~!
Please tell me if he sings again!

EIGHTY YEARS...
I HAVE TO LIVE THAT LONG...

IN THE PROCESS OF LEARNING WORDS...
COULD IT BE THAT YOU'RE STILL VERY YOUNG?

MANMERUN~! UWAZUMUNE~! SO SAD~! ANOTHER ONE!
HUH?!
H-HE SANG AGAIN?!
SWAY
SWAY
HE DEFINITELY SANG! I CAN'T BELIEVE HE REMEMBERED SO MANY WORDS!
UM... WHAT DID HE SAY AGAIN...?
"MARUME RUN"? "UWAZUMU"...?
Indianacrow @Indianacrow
Niji sang again. "Manmerun, Uwazumune. So sad, Another one."
......
WHAT KIND OF SONG IS THIS?
OH, I GOT A LIKE...

LA...
LA...

LA LA LA~!
H-HE STARTED SINGING AGAIN?!

DIRTY JOOKS RIGHT?
DON'T THEY SAY. OFTEN?
WELL, THAT'S~?
HEY. HEY. HEY.
HEEEEEY?
EH LA LA LA LA
MM...GYU!
WITH YOU.

DIRTY JOO... "DIRTY JOKES, RIGHT?
DON'T THEY SAY, OFTEN?" ...?
"WELL, THAT'S" ...?

......
WHAT IS THIS?!
Indianacrow @Indianacr
Niji sang this:
Don't they often say dirty
Well, that's.
Hey. Hey. Hey.
Heeeeey.
Eh la la la la
Gyu!
With you."
It seems.
H, I
OT A
IKE...

HEY, NIJI-CHAN.
WHAT KIND OF SONG WAS IT?
SING.
NIJI SANG?!
I WANT TO HEAR IT, TOO! WHAT DID HE SING?!
AM I NOT GOOD ENOUGH, AFTER ALL?
HE JUST SUDDENLY STARTED SINGING. IT'S COMPLETELY UNPREDICT-ABLE!
I WANTED TO TAKE A VIDEO OF IT.
YOU SHOULD HAVE THE CAMERA READY AT ALL TIMES!

SNORT...
SNORT...
SWAY...
SWAY...
IS IT HAPPEN-ING?!
OH!
SILENT...
THIS IS SURPRISINGLY FRUSTRATING.
WHY DON'T YOU JUST GO AND TAKE A BATH?
I GUESS IT WON'T HAPPEN UNLESS HE'S IN A GOOD MOOD...
I'LL GO START THE BATH.

TING-ALING-ALING LING LING. ♪ YOUR BATH... ♪ IS READY!
I HAVEN'T PUSHED THE BUTTON YET.
HAAH! I GOT IT!
OH! THE BATH NOTIFICA-TION...!
THAT WAS NIJI!
HIS MIMICRY WAS REALLY CONFUSING.
I GOT IT! I GOT IT!

TING-ALING TING-ALING! ♪
TING-ALING LING! ♪
THIS...
I WONDER IF I CAN PUT IT UP ON TWEETER.
I WANT NANA-CHAN'S OWNER TO SEE IT.
I WONDER IF NANA-CHAN DOES THINGS LIKE THIS, TOO.
I'LL POST IT.
I HOPE NANA-CHAN AND LARC-SAN SEE IT.
IT'S NICE THAT I ONLY HAVE TWO FOLLOWERS.

PA-
PING
PA-
PING
HM
?!
PA-
PING

PA-PING
PA-PING
AHHHH.
UWAA-ARGH...
HA HA.
SO, THIS IS THE RUMORED ...
"SHOOT, THE VIEWS WON'T STOP," EFFECT...
AH HA HA. NO, NO.
YOU'RE A TWEETER USER?
HOW UNLIKE YOU.
A-A LOT OF THINGS HAPPENED.

WELL, YOU DIDN'T POST ANY PERSONAL INFORMATION.
IT'LL PROBABLY BE FINE, RIGHT?
IT'S *NOT* FINE.
PEOPLE HAVE ALREADY STARTED REPOSTING THE VIDEO WITHOUT MY PERMISSION.
Handpicked ★ Cute Video
My Bird is a Water Heater♪
UWA HA HA. STOP. DON'T GIVE IT A TITLE LIKE THAT.
HE'S NOT *YOUR* BIRD. HE'S *MY* BIRD.
Indianacrow
Replying: @dskg93etvj55
You are reposting my video without permission.
This is the original tweet.
https://tubuyaiter.com/woijg_fhf/status
iuhfiikjh26a @oij2125dssdff
Replying: @Indianacrow
You allowed reposting the moment you poste
that video on the net. Stupid.
What kind of animal is this?
I've never seen it before.
PLEASE DON'T SAY MALICIOUS THINGS. YOU'RE THE ONE WHO'S STUPID. PLEASE STOP.
Late Night Fluffy TV Coverage Team
Replying: @Indianacrow
OX TV's "Late Night Fluffy TV" would like to use your video on this week's show. May we get permission to use this video?
KGFGetOK @ksjfjov6
Sounds just like mine.
I DON'T KNOW. I HAVE NO IDEA HOW TO RESPOND. DEFINITELY NOT.
I CAN'T JUST DELETE MY TWEET, RIGHT...?
I'VE GOT TO KEEP THINGS BLACK AND WHITE...KEEP THINGS BLACK AND WHITE!

KEEP THINGS BLACK AND WHITE...
FWP
FWP
BLACK AND WHITE...
KEEP IT...
PA-PHOONK

Rainbow and Black
Story & Art by Eri Takenashi

NOW LOADING...

#9 Solace

Trends >

AH... AWARGH...

What is this strange animal? The "happy mouse" everyone is talking about on the internet.
> Read more...

SIZZ

I-I ENDED UP MAKING THEM FAMOUS...

BLACK AND WHITE... I CAN'T SET THINGS STRAIGHT IN BLACK AND WHITE.

Nana @n
I'm hung

NANA-SAN... PLEASE HELP ME... IS IT OKAY IF I GET SOME ADVICE FROM HER?

Nana @nanac
My nails right now.

HER NAILS ARE CUTE.

Sorry for the sudden DM. I am having some problems with the huge number of retweets. What should I do? I don't want TV or news channels to use my video.

Indianacrow

Thank you for the DM. It's trending really high right now~! You don't have to respond to all the replies. And I think just saying, "No, thank you." is enough for the media companies.

Nana

PA-PING

Was it bad for me to retweet this?! If so, I'm so very sorry!

Nana

No, it's my fault for not understanding how social media works and getting a little uncomfortable over something I wasn't prepared for. I was very happy that you retweeted my post.

Indianacrow

Ahh~! I'm so sorry~!
I didn't think that things would get so out of hand. It's your first time so it must have come as quite a surprise! I'm the type that gets pretty happy when I get retweeted, so I didn't think of your feelings at all. I am very sorry.

Nana

I ENDED UP MAKING NANA-SAN FEEL BAD ...!

"NO, IT WAS JUST THAT I DIDN'T REALLY UNDER-STAND."

AND SEND...

AH...

I MADE THINGS AWKWARD BETWEEN US...

AHH...
AAH...
Nuzzle ♥

NUZZLE
NUZZLE

NUZZLE
HUH ...?

WHY ARE YOU MOVING LIKE THAT...?
DO YOU WANT ATTENTION...?
NUZZLE

COULD IT BE THAT YOU'RE...

TRYING TO CHEER ME UP?

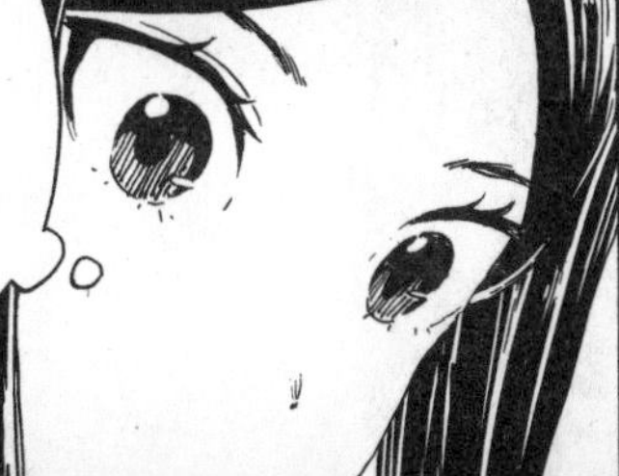

HE'S NEVER DONE ANYTHING LIKE THIS BEFORE.

NUZZLE
MAU MAU.
HUH?
WHAAAAAT?!
MAU MAU.
OH MY GOSH!

THE LOVE FROM AN ANIMAL.
PRICE-LESS...

I'M OKAY NOW.

WHAM

1 Tachikawa-kita
Kamikitadai Station

Nana @nanachan0521
I want a calendar from
I'm going to buy curry,

Nana @nanachan0521
s been a long time since
Tama Center; it's change

na @nanachan0521
ly I've gotten really seriou
I'll try to make this. ↓

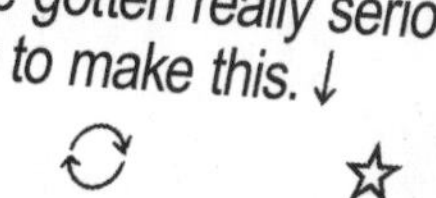

OH.

PA-DING★

You have a new DM!

I've gotten more followers, but I don't really want them.

Indianacrow 

Then why don't you change your account to a locked account?

 Nana

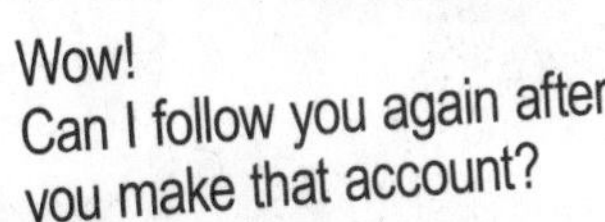
Wow!
Can I follow you again after you make that account?
PA-PING★

Nana
Of course. That's the reason I'm making the account.

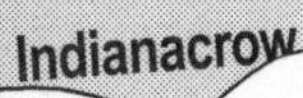
Indianacrow
WHAT THE HECK?
I SHOULD HAVE DONE THIS FROM THE BEGINNING.

PA-PING★

THUMP
THUMP
THUMP
THUMP

WAIT.
WAIT, KUROE.
I WANT TO TALK TO HER...
BUT SHE MAY NOT FEEL THE SAME WAY.
SOME PEOPLE ARE SCARED OF MEETING PEOPLE FROM THE INTERNET IN REAL LIFE.
TO BEGIN WITH, IT'D BE CREEPY SINCE I KNEW WE LIVED NEAR EACH OTHER.
AND WHAT IF SHE WASN'T EVEN THE RIGHT PERSON AT ALL?

GASP
PA-DING★
I can't wait. ☆
Nana

多摩センター
Tama Center
Tama Center

ARE YOU... "NANA"-SAN?
I AM "INDIANA-CROW."

I SAID IT.
YOU'RE SUCH A BEAUTY!

HUH ?!
NO, THAT'S NOT...
YOU'RE MUCH MORE...
I THOUGHT YOU WERE A GUY!
BUT YOU'RE A SERIOUS BEAUTY!
HOW'D YOU KNOW IT WAS ME?!
YOUR NAILS...
OH!
I SEE! MY NAILS!

HOW DID YOU KNOW IT WAS ME, NANA-SAN?
I NEVER TWEET ANY PERSONAL INFORMATION...
YOU GOT YOUR LOCATION SETTING ON.
?!
OH, I GUESS YOU DIDN'T NOTICE.
AFTER THE LAST COUPLE OF UPDATES, IT CAN BE SEEN FROM YOUR MESSAGES.
I... DIDN'T KNOW.
SO SCARY...
IT REALLY IS!
THOSE SUDDEN USER CHANGES.
I NOTICED YOU LIVED REALLY CLOSE TO ME...
SO I WAS HOPING WE'D MEET UP.

ME TOO.
I THOUGHT MAYBE WE'D BUMP INTO EACH OTHER.
GOT SOME FREE TIME NOW?
INSTEAD OF STANDING AROUND...
LET'S GO GET SOME TEA!
Rainbow and Black (1) END

SPECIAL THANKS

Informational Help: Kakegawa Kachouen

STAFF: Haseyoshi Eria

SEVEN SEAS ENTERTAINMENT PRESENTS

Rainbow and Black

story and art by ERI TAKENASHI

VOLUME 1

TRANSLATION
Angela Liu

ADAPTATION
Sam Mitchell

LETTERING AND RETOUCH
Ochie Caraan

COVER DESIGN
K.C. Fabellon

PROOFREADER
Dawn Davis

EDITOR
Shanti Whitesides

PREPRESS TECHNICIAN
Rhiannon Rasmussen-Silverstein

PRODUCTION MANAGER
Lissa Pattillo

MANAGING EDITOR
Julie Davis

ASSOCIATE PUBLISHER
Adam Arnold

PUBLISHER
Jason DeAngelis

NIJI TO KURO VOL.1

First published in Japan in 2019 by Ichijinsha Inc., Tokyo.
Publication rights for this English edition arranged through Kodansha Ltd., Tokyo.

Seven Seas press and purchase enquiries can be sent to Marketing Manager Lianne Sentar at press@gomanga.com. Information regarding the distribution and purchase of digital editions is available from Digital Manager CK Russell at digital@gomanga.com.

ISBN: 978-1-64505-840-3

Printed in Canada

First Printing: November 2020

10 9 8 7 6 5 4 3 2 1

READING DIRECTIONS

This book reads from ***right to left***, Japanese style. If this is your first time reading manga, you start reading from the top right panel on each page and take it from there. If you get lost, just follow the numbered diagram here. It may seem backwards at first, but you'll get the hang of it! Have fun!!

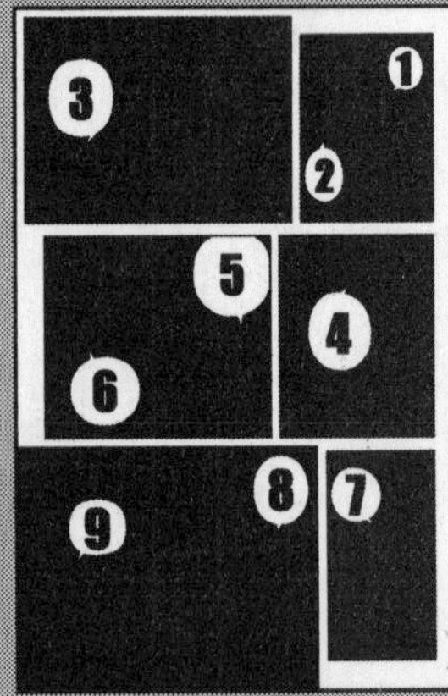